PAPA CAN!

DIANA ROBINSON
& the Shovlin FAMILY

Transformed Publishing

Mission: To Proclaim Transformation and Truth

Publisher: Transformed Publishing, Cocoa, FL

Website: www.transformedpublishing.com

Email: transformedpublishing@gmail.com

ISBN: 978-1-953241-45-0

Dedicated
To Every
Papa Who CAN & DOES!

Continue to invest your wisdom, perseverance, service, skill, and LOVE as an inheritance to your family & friends. They will continue to build on the foundation you intentionally instill.

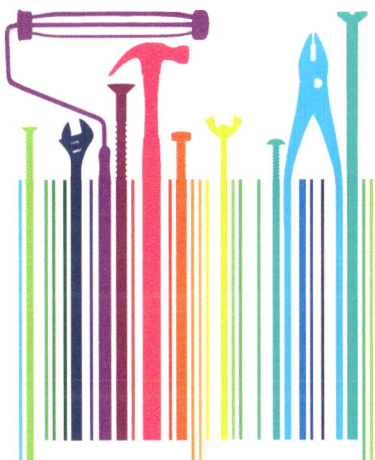

I can't reach it.

It's too high.

Papa can!

Papa can reach everything.

I can't fix it.

It's too broken.

Papa can!

Papa can fix everything.

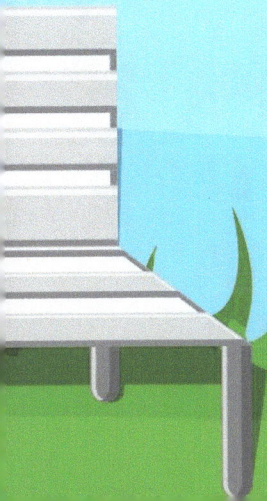

I can't drive it.

It's too big.

Papa can!

Papa can drive everything.

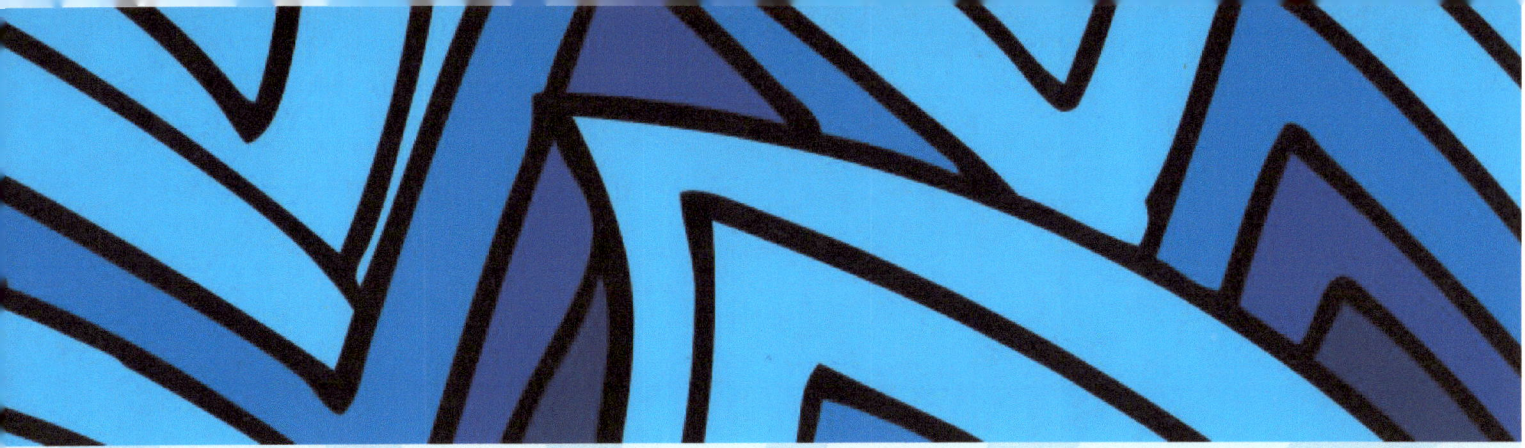

I can't play it.

It's too difficult.

Papa can!

Papa can play everything.

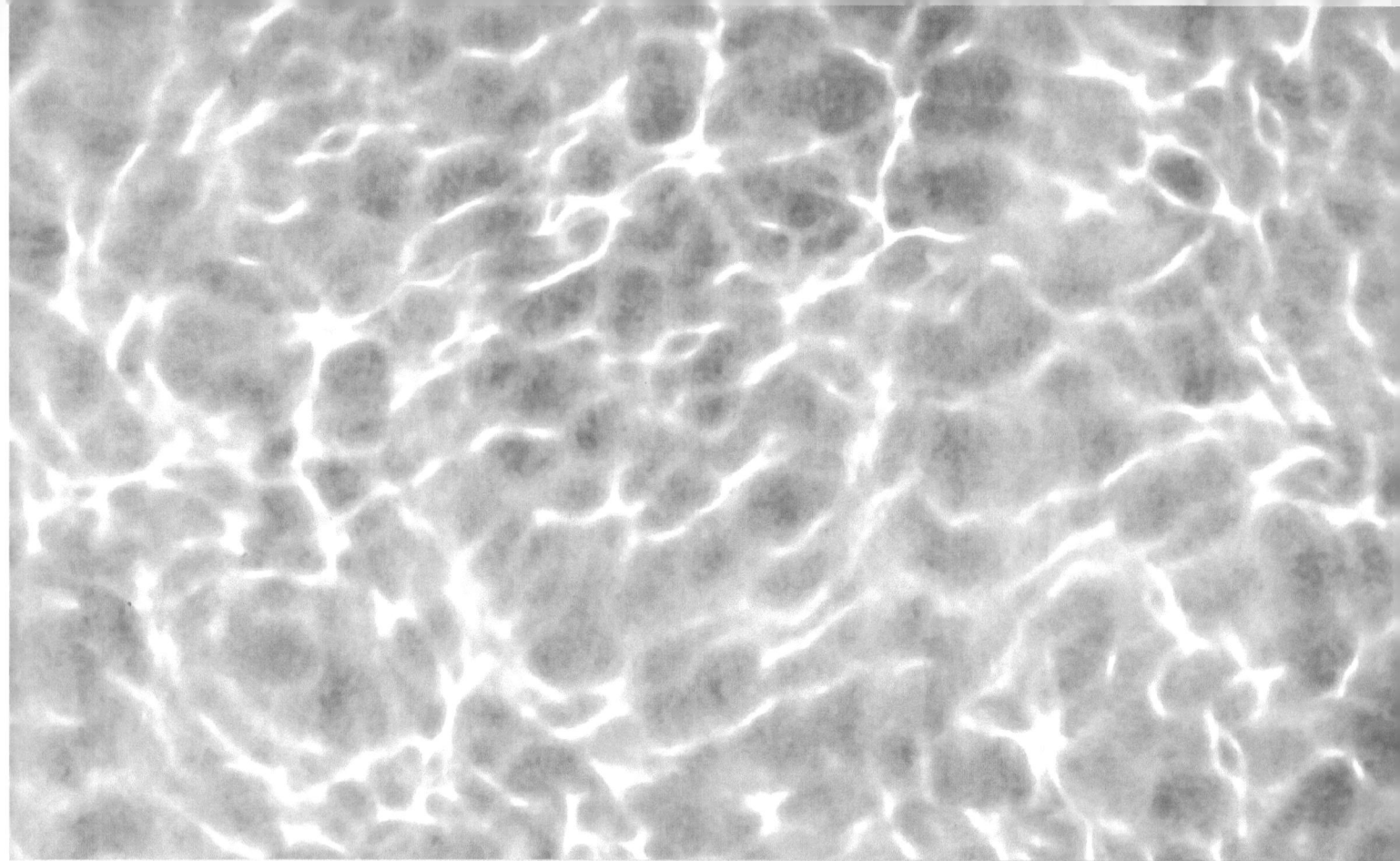

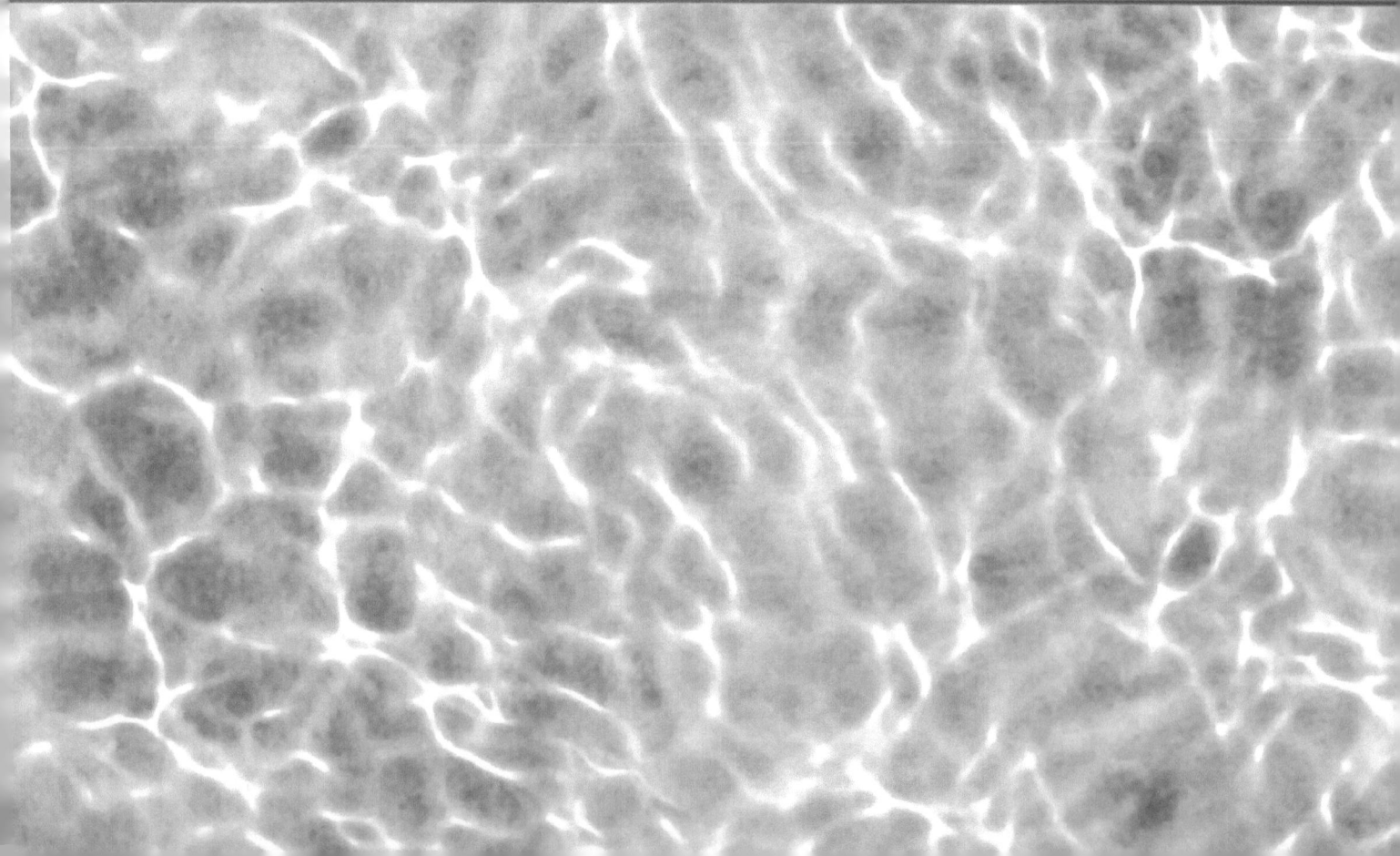

I can't swim across the pool. It's too far.

Papa can!

Papa can teach me to do everything I can't.

I can't ride a bike.
It's too wobbly.

Papa can!

Papa can teach me to do
everything I can't.

I can't read a book.

It's too hard.

Papa can!

Papa can teach me to do everything I can't.

ZOOM
WHAP!
CRASH!
HELP!
KA-BOOM!
WOOF
SLOPPYKISSES
DOG
RUFF
RUFF
RUFF
TREATS
SQUEAKY
TOY
Dog House
FIFI
GOOD DOG

I can't buy it.
It's too expensive.

Papa can!

Papa can help me buy
everything I can't.

I can't bounce it.
It's too flat.

Papa can inflate it!

He's always ready to help.
Papa does what I need,
when I need it!

I can't eat it.

It's too sweet.

Papa tells my parents I can!

He's always ready to help.

Papa does what I need, when I need it!

Papa is there for everything!
He's always ready to say, "Good Job!"

Papa can always make me smile
and loves to hear me laugh.

Papa never pushes me
to be anything—
Papa supports me
to be everything!

Papa can't use his cell phone.

It's too frustrating.

I can!

Papa taught me so much,
and I can teach him too.

Papa will still do it!
When I am a kid or an adult,

FANS

PAPA CAN!

TILE

BACKSPLASH

PAINTING

FAUCETS

FUSE BOXES

WOOD TRIM

TOILETS

INSIDE!

LIGHT SWITCHES

ELECTRIC SOCKETS

WASHERS

DRYERS

REFRIGERATORS, FREEZERS, & ICE MACHINES

LAMINATE FLOORS

TREES

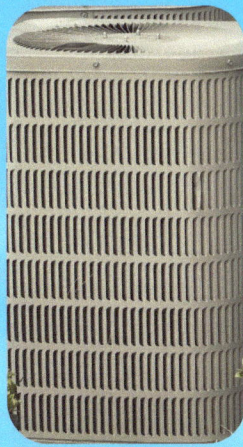

AIR CONDITIONERS

SPRINKLERS

SWING SETS

ROOFS

OUTSIDE!

POOLS

All this, is just a little bit of what PAPA CAN do!

FENCES

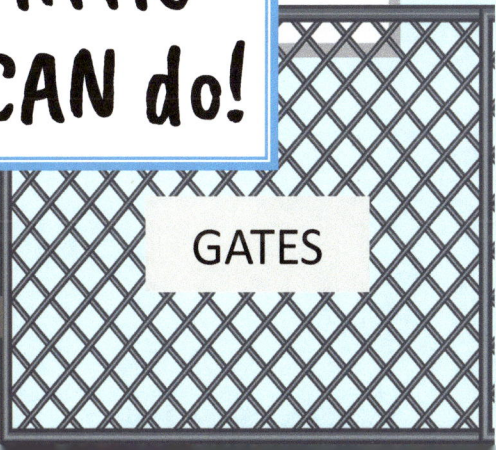

GATES

Reach it! Fix it!
Drive it! Play it!
Teach it! Buy it!
Inflate it! Build it!
And so much more!
PAPA CAN
& PAPA WILL!

"Papa, you buy it—you build it!"

But, Papa won't . . .

change any diapers!

Special Acknowledgement to Our Papa

Live with PURPOSE

Don't put off what you can do today . . .
Respond to the call & *'take a ride over'*!

Infuse the life of your loved ones with
your sincere love & God-given talents!

Never push anyone to be anything—
Support them to be *everything*!

**Keys of Life Lived
by John Charles Shovlin
7/6/53—4/17/23 to Eternity**

Let Your work appear
to Your servants, and
Your glory to their children.
And let the beauty of the
Lord our God be upon us,
And establish the work
of our hands for us;
Yes, establish the
work of our hands.
-Psalm 90:16-17